AF271271

Dirty Jobs

Taxidermist

Simon Rose

www.av2books.com

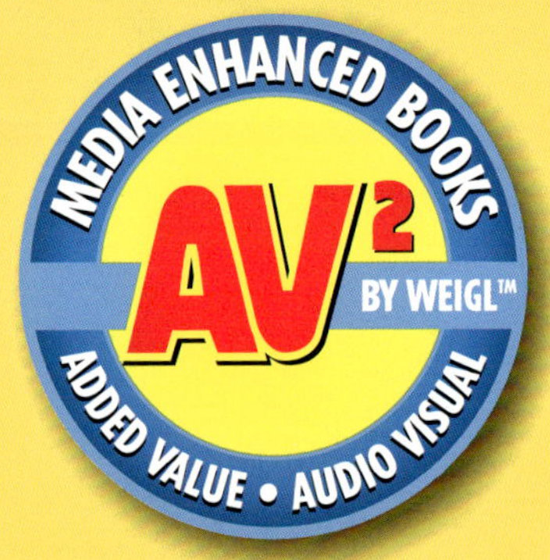

AV² provides enriched content that supplements and complements this book. Weigl's AV² books strive to create inspired learning and engage young minds in a total learning experience.

Your AV² Media Enhanced books come alive with...

Go to **www.av2books.com**, and enter this book's unique code.

BOOK CODE

T565238

AV² by Weigl brings you media enhanced books that support active learning.

Audio
Listen to sections of the book read aloud.

Key Words
Study vocabulary, and complete a matching word activity.

Video
Watch informative video clips.

Quizzes
Test your knowledge.

Embedded Weblinks
Gain additional information for research.

Slide Show
View images and captions, and prepare a presentation.

Try This!
Complete activities and hands-on experiments.

... and much, much more!

Published by AV² by Weigl
350 5th Avenue, 59th Floor
New York, NY 10118

Websites: www.av2books.com www.weigl.com

Library of Congress Control Number: 2014934857

ISBN 978-1-4896-1006-5 (hardcover)
ISBN 978-1-4896-1007-2 (softcover)
ISBN 978-1-4896-1008-9 (single-user eBook)
ISBN 978-1-4896-1009-6 (multi-user eBook)

Printed in the United States of America in Brainerd, Minnesota
1 2 3 4 5 6 7 8 9 0 19 18 17 16 15

012015
WEP051214

Senior Editor: Aaron Carr
Designer: Mandy Christiansen

Every reasonable effort has been made to trace ownership and to obtain permission to reprint copyright material. The publishers would be pleased to have any errors or omissions brought to their attention so that they may be corrected in subsequent printings.

Weigl acknowledges Getty Images as its primary image supplier for this title.

Contents

What Is a Taxidermist?

axidermy is the art of preserving animals by keeping the skins, fur, feathers, and scales to make lifelike replicas. Taxidermists typically **preserve** such animals as birds, fish, mammals, and reptiles. Scientists and other professionals use these realistic models to study animals. People also use them for decoration. Museums display the models in exhibits, while some people feature them in private home collections. Professional taxidermists undergo training. Their work may involve casting, **molding**, and woodworking. Taxidermists usually also have artistic skills in drawing, painting, or sculpting.

Taxidermy Terms

The word taxidermy comes from two Greek words. These are *taxis*, meaning "arrangement," and *derma*, meaning "skin." Taxidermists do not refer to completed **specimens** as being "stuffed." The correct term is "mounted." They also refer to skins as "**hides**." People in the 17th and 18th centuries mounted animals by placing their hides over their skeletons and filling them with straw or wood shavings.

The oldest mounted specimen is a **400-year-old** rhinoceros in Florence, Italy.

A taxidermist is a professional who works in the taxidermy field.

Where They Work

A taxidermist might work in a taxidermy shop at the beginning of his or her career. While working in a shop, new taxidermists learn the art of the job as they train with experienced professionals. They also work in sports shops that specialize in hunting and fishing. There, taxidermists would mostly work on creating hunting trophies of mammals, birds, and fish. Some taxidermists open shops on their own or start taxidermy businesses from their homes.

Taxidermists may attempt to recreate an animal without using any of its actual parts when taking part in taxidermy competitions.

Working in Museums

Some taxidermists may work at **natural history museums**. Their job is to create lifelike replicas of animals for museum exhibits and displays. These can be examples of individual animals or groups of the same animal. Taxidermists may also create **habitat** displays. These show museum visitors how the animals live in the wild.

Taxidermists must make replicas of grasses and other natural surroundings to make a habitat exhibit more realistic.

A Dirty Job

Taxidermists work with large and small animals that have recently died. Taxidermists must be comfortable with seeing the internal parts of animals, including their organs and muscle tissues. They remove an animal's skin by making small cuts with very sharp blades. This can involve a lot of blood. They must remove the skin very carefully and slowly so they do not damage it. Taxidermists also have to clean the skin once they pull it off the animal's body. This involves scraping the inside of the skin to remove any fat or attached muscle. Taxidermists also have to remove the animal's eyes and other soft tissue. They will later replace these with human-made materials.

Tanning and Preserving

Tanning is a complex process that preserves the animal's skin and stops it from rotting. Taxidermists must begin this process right after removing the skin from the animal's body. They place salt on the skins before hanging them to dry. After washing the salt off and drying the skins again, they soak the skins in chemicals. Taxidermists wear safety clothing, because many chemicals can be dangerous if they contact human skin. Taxidermists must also wear gloves when rubbing tanning oils into the animal's hide.

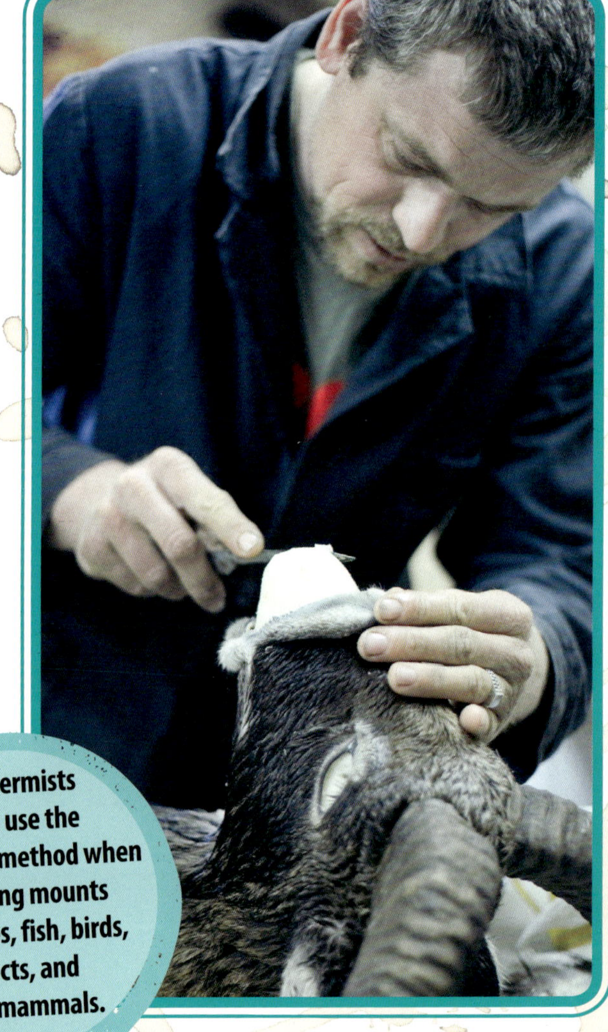

Taxidermists often use the freeze-dry method when preparing mounts of reptiles, fish, birds, insects, and small mammals.

Taxidermist

Taxidermy is not that popular a profession, but there are still many people who choose this as a career. Some taxidermists are registered with professional organizations, while others do taxidermy only as a hobby. As a result, it is difficult to determine the exact number of people employed in the profession.

More than

75,000

The number of taxidermists believed to be working in the United States.

$2,000

Costs and work times vary, but this would be the average minimum price a taxidermist would charge to mount a full-size adult bear in a standing pose.

$500 to $650

The average price of a mounted deer.

6 to 9 months

All taxidermists are different, but a quality mount typically takes this long to complete.

Taxidermists can often use an animal's real antlers when preparing the mount.

Hides must be stored in a cool, dry place to preserve the quality of the animals' skin.

All in a Day's Work

Once the taxidermist finishes preparing the skin, he or she places it on a **form**. This is an accurate sculpture of the animal. The form includes the shape of all muscles, so it requires careful attention. The taxidermist must stretch the hide over the form to make sure it fits correctly. When he or she is satisfied, the taxidermist fastens the skin to the form with thread and glue. This is when the artistic part of the process begins. The taxidermist adds artificial parts, such as the eyes and soft tissues. He or she may use paint to restore faded colors, especially with fish, or add artificial teeth and claws to mammal or bird specimens. Some taxidermists may also prepare other natural material for museum displays or exhibits. These include trees, plants, leaves, and soils.

Sculptures and Forms

Taxidermists usually make their forms or sculptures in realistic poses. For example, they often show birds in flight and stage lions in hunting positions. Taxidermists can purchase their own forms, but many prefer to make their own. There are many ways to do this. Taxidermists can cover a wire frame with clay, or they can build them from wood or foam. Sometimes, a taxidermist uses the animal's skeleton or other parts to construct the form. Some taxidermists create a plaster cast of the animal's body after they remove the skin and use it as a mold.

Artificial Parts

Taxidermists use many artificial parts when making a mounted animal. They use glass for the eyes and clay for the eyelids. Other materials common in taxidermy are wax and epoxy, a type of **resin**. They use these for the soft tissues of the lips, mouth, or nose.

Game Heads

Game heads are the most popular mounts that taxidermists create. These specimens feature only the head, neck, and shoulders of an animal. Most game heads are of deer, elk, and pronghorn antelope, but taxidermists also mount other animals in this way.

Staying Safe

Taxidermists face many hazards while working. They handle knives and other very sharp objects and use dangerous chemicals and **solutions**. Taxidermists wear certain types of clothing and use safety equipment as a precaution.

Fleshing Gloves

Fleshing gloves protect the taxidermist from accidental cuts. Fleshing gloves are made of Kevlar, a tough fiber also used to make body armor. The gloves have longer cuffs to prevent wrist injuries. They also have flat grip dots to help the taxidermist keep hold of slippery animals.

Apron

Aprons are usually made of plastic or rubber. They cover the lower part of the body and much of the chest while a taxidermist works. Aprons protect the wearer from acids, alcohol, grease, oils, and many different chemicals. Aprons are easy to clean and can be used again.

Safety Glasses

Taxidermists work with solutions that can irritate or damage the eyes. They wear sturdy safety glasses that have a tight seal around the face. The glasses can have either glass or plastic lenses, and they have a strap for adjusting the size.

Latex Gloves

Latex gloves are disposable, very lightweight, and easily conform to the shape of the wearer's hand. The gloves help protect the taxidermist from chemicals and other harmful liquids used to clean and preserve the animal hides.

Tools of the Trade

In addition to safety clothing and equipment, taxidermists use special tools in their work. They use sharp instruments to remove the hide and any remaining animal tissue. They keep various chemicals and solutions in special containers for added safety. Taxidermists also use needles, thread, brushes, and cloths after they complete the mounting.

Cutting Tools

Taxidermists use various bladed tools in their work. These include **utility blades**, fleshing tools, knives, scissors, **scalpels**, and sharpened spoons. The blades of these tools are very sharp. This makes it easier to remove an animal's skin from its body. Taxidermists use sharp spoons and fleshing tools to carefully scrape the inside of the skin to remove any pieces of muscle tissue. Taxidermists select the type of knife or other tool based on the size and shape of the animal. Some animals have skin that tears easily, so taxidermists need a very delicate blade, while other skin types are tougher.

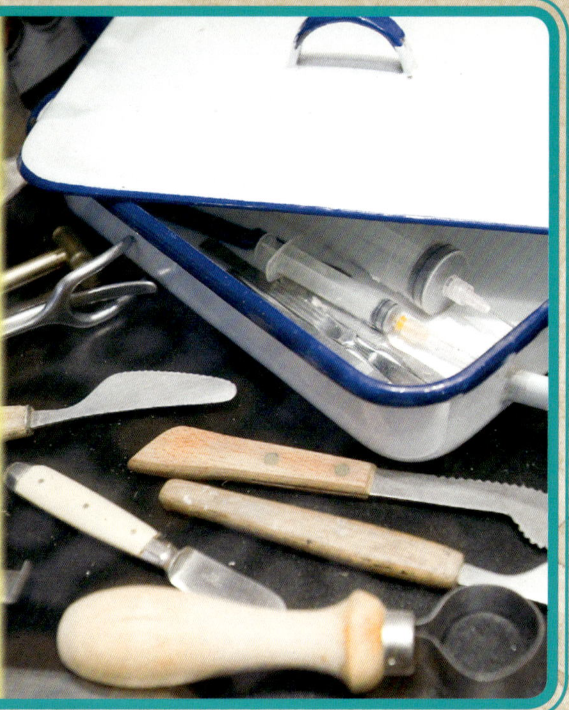

Brushes

After the mounting is completed, taxidermists use brushes or cloths to make a mammal's coat look realistic. They might use toothbrushes or combs on a bird's feathers or even clean an animal's teeth if needed. Taxidermists often need to paint fish in order to retain any bright colors they had when alive.

Plastic Containers

Taxidermists use a number of solutions in the **tanning** process. They have plastic buckets, bowls, and other containers as well as measuring cups. They use these to hold the different solutions and to clean tools and other instruments. Taxidermists must keep the solutions separate and label them carefully to prevent accidents. Some of the liquids can be dangerous if people mix them together.

Glue

Taxidermists use glue during the mounting process to fasten glass eyes into the sockets and to secure any loose teeth. Taxidermists often use a **caulking** gun to apply the glue. They make sure the glue is not visible once it dries.

Needle and Thread

Taxidermists use a needle and thread after the tanning process. Needles must be strong enough to go through the animal's hide. The needle size depends on the project. For example, taxidermists use smaller needles on areas where they do not want to see the hole. They use strong thread, such as fishing line or even dental floss, to hold the skin together.

The Taxidermist's Role

Today's taxidermists work in many different areas, such as carpentry, molding, casting, and sculpting. Some taxidermists who run their own businesses may not perform skinning and tanning themselves. Tanning requires a large work area, and taxidermists may send the skin to a separate tanning shop. Taxidermists with their own shops perform a variety of work. Museums or educational institutions may ask them to preserve animals, or they may produce hunting trophies. Some animal lovers even ask taxidermists to preserve their pets.

Prices for mounts vary and depend on the size of the animal and the pose created. The mounting process can take anywhere from two or three months to a year, depending on the size of the animal and the taxidermist's workload. They are very busy preserving fish in spring and summer, and they spend a lot of time on deer and other large mammals in the fall.

Fish Models

Taxidermists often create saltwater fish mounts using artificial material rather than natural parts. Anglers often catch and release the fish, so taxidermists can create a realistic trophy using accurate measurements and photographs.

Fish mounting is difficult because it involves many small details. This includes reproducing the many bright colors of the fish.

Becoming a Taxidermist

Taxidermists are artists, and the work they produce can command high prices. Skilled taxidermists can be very much in demand and run successful businesses. To become a taxidermist, you need to have interests and knowledge in specific areas. You will need to study the anatomy of animals, as well as their habits and behavior. Consider learning techniques of casting, molding, and woodworking. Brush up on your art skills, as you also need to have some artistic ability with painting or drawing, especially of animals.

Taxidermist Salaries

A taxidermist's salary is usually about $40,000 per year, but salaries vary from place to place. Taxidermists who work in museums or for educational institutions are paid a monthly salary for their work. Taxidermists make more money in larger cities than in smaller towns. Taxidermists who have their own businesses have high costs due to the expensive materials they need. These include mounting supplies, art supplies, and chemicals. These costs can amount to more than 50 percent of a taxidermist's income. Taxidermists also tend to be busy only at certain times of the year, such as during or just after hunting seasons.

Taxidermists also charge different fees for mounting animals. Taxidermists who are very skilled and have a good reputation can command a higher fee. The size of the animal and the requested pose affect the costs of mounting services.

There are no formal education requirements to become a taxidermist, but many schools offer specialized training programs.

Is This Career for You?

Taxidermy careers are not for everyone. Even if you have some or all of the skills required, you might be uncomfortable working with dead animals. If you feel this way during your early training, the feeling is unlikely to go away and you may need to consider a different career. Most taxidermists enter the profession with the aim of operating their own business, rather than working for a museum or a similar organization. If you hope to run your own taxidermy shop, you will also need to know about self-employment and business management.

Interests

If you are interested in animals and the habits and habitats of wildlife, you should consider taking carpentry or sculpting classes. You can also take courses to improve your artistic skills.

Training and Education

Colleges and trade schools often provide taxidermy courses. Training usually involves hands-on experience with professional taxidermists. You may also wish to study business and marketing if you plan to operate your own shop.

Licenses and Certificates

Licensing can vary in different parts of the country. In some areas, you may need to take exams or obtain licenses specifically related to fish, mammals, or birds. You can also obtain professional certification with the National Taxidermists Association (NTA), which can help you to build your business.

Career Connections

Plan your taxidermist career with this activity. Follow the instructions outlined in the steps to complete the process of becoming an taxidermist.

1. Speak to a taxidermist in your community. This person can tell you about taxidermy. He or she can also answer your questions about the job.

2. Visit a job fair or a university career center to learn about working in the taxidermy industry.

4. Call or write to a taxidermy company. Say that you are interested in a taxidermy position. Ask for advice on how to apply.

3. Work on your resumé. A good resumé that shows your strongest skills can go a long way toward attracting the attention of potential employers.

1. Visit local taxidermy shops. Explain that you are very interested in their work, and be sure to ask questions. See if you can get a tour of the shop or, better still, see a taxidermist at work.

2. Study how to draw animals and learn about animal biology from books and websites. Watch instructional videos, and visit websites about taxidermy.

3. If possible, obtain an apprenticeship. Working with an experienced taxidermist will help you decide if this career is for you.

4. Apply to a college and enroll in taxidermy courses, where you can learn the latest techniques.

5. Learn about the licensing laws for taxidermists in your area. These will vary from place to place.

Quiz

1. What does NTA stand for?

2. What equipment do taxidermists use to scrape the inside of the animal's skin?

3. From what language does the word *taxidermy* originate?

4. How do taxidermists apply glue?

5. What are the eyes of a completed animal specimen made of?

6. At what time of year do taxidermists do most of their work?

7. What is tanning?

8. What tools might a taxidermist use on a bird's feathers?

9. What were mounted animals filled with during the 17th and 18th centuries?

10. What are the most popular mounts that taxidermists create?

Answers: 1. National Taxidermists Association **2.** Sharp spoons and fleshing tools **3.** Greek **4.** With a glue or caulking gun **5.** Glass **6.** During or just after hunting seasons **7.** The process that preserves an animal's skin and stops it from rotting **8.** Toothbrushes or combs **9.** Straw or wood shavings **10.** Game heads

Key Words

caulking: a waterproof filler and sealant

fleshing: removing tissue from a hide

form: a sculpture of an animal used by taxidermists

game heads: animal mounts that consist of the head, neck, and shoulders only

habitat: the natural environment of an organism or species

hides: another word for the skins of animals

latex: a rubber material used to make gloves and other products

molding: creating a frame or model over which something else can be shaped

natural history museums: museums that focus on the subject of natural history, including animals

preserve: to keep something in its original state or condition

resin: a sticky material used to make a wide range of products

scalpels: small, straight knives with sharp, thin blades; used by medical professionals for surgery and dissection

solutions: mixtures of two or more substances

specimens: typical animals or plants that serve as samples of a substance or material for study

tanning: a process that preserves an animal's skin

utility blades: sharp, replaceable blades that can be retracted into the handle of a knife

Index

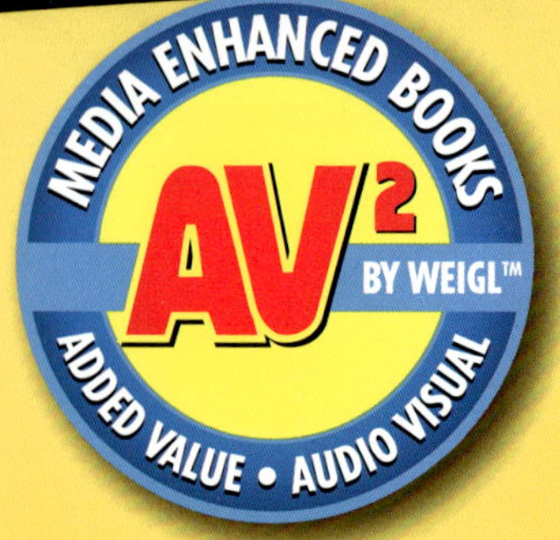

Log on to www.av2books.com

AV² by Weigl brings you media enhanced books that support active learning. Go to www.av2books.com, and enter the special code found on page 2 of this book. You will gain access to enriched and enhanced content that supplements and complements this book. Content includes video, audio, weblinks, quizzes, a slide show, and activities.

AV² Online Navigation

Audio
Listen to sections of the book read aloud.

Book Pages
AV² pages directly correspond to pages in the book.

Video
Watch informative video clips.

Key Words
Study vocabulary, and complete a matching word activity.

Embedded Weblinks
Gain additional information for research.

Quizzes
Test your knowledge.

Slide Show
View images and captions, and prepare a presentation.

Try This!
Complete activities and hands-on experiments.

AV² was built to bridge the gap between print and digital. We encourage you to tell us what you like and what you want to see in the future.

Sign up to be an AV² Ambassador at www.av2books.com/ambassador.

Due to the dynamic nature of the Internet, some of the URLs and activities provided as part of AV² by Weigl may have changed or ceased to exist. AV² by Weigl accepts no responsibility for any such changes. All media enhanced books are regularly monitored to update addresses and sites in a timely manner. Contact AV² by Weigl at 1-866-649-3445 or av2books@weigl.com with any questions, comments, or feedback.